Amazing Arachnids

By Lucy Floyd

Celebration Press
Pearson Learning Group

Contents

A Spider's Body

Spiders vary greatly in size. Some are the size of a tiny dot, while others are larger than your hand. Most spiders are brown, gray, or black. Some, however, are white, yellow, or even green.

Because spiders have legs, you might think they have leg bones. In fact, spiders have no bones at all. What they do have is a very tough skin, an outer skeleton, which protects their bodies and legs. Many spiders are hairy and bumpy, too.

Spiders have eight legs and two main body parts.

Along with eight legs, spiders often have eight eyes. Hunting spiders, which chase and catch their prey, can see quite well. Web-weaving spiders, which catch their prey in webs, generally have poor vision.

The front part of a spider's body, a combined head and chest, is called the cephalothorax (sef uh loh THOR aks). *Cephalo* comes from a Greek word meaning "head," and *thorax* comes from a Greek word meaning "chest." The back part of a spider's body is called the abdomen. Look at the chart below to compare the parts of an insect's body with those of a spider's body.

INSECT	SPIDER
head thorax } ⟶	cephalothorax
abdomen	abdomen
six legs	eight legs

Spinning Silk

All spiders can do something amazing. They can produce silk threads. The glands for making silk are in the spider's abdomen and are connected to organs called **spinnerets**. Liquid silk comes out of little tubes on the spinnerets. Once out in the air, it hardens into a thread. Some—but not all—spiders use the silk to spin webs.

This spider's dragline is attached to a leaf.

Spiders could not live without silk. When spiders move around, they pull a line of silk called a **dragline** behind them. It keeps them from falling. Spiders can also use it to drop down to the ground to escape from enemies. A dragline is a "lifeline" for spiders!

Weaving Webs

Spiders use silk in many different ways. Some line underground burrows with it. Others line a folded leaf with silk to make a nest.

Weaving a web is one of the most amazing things spiders do with silk. Spider webs are like snowflakes—no two are exactly alike. Web-weaving spiders do not have to "learn" how to weave these wondrous webs. Young spiders know how without being taught.

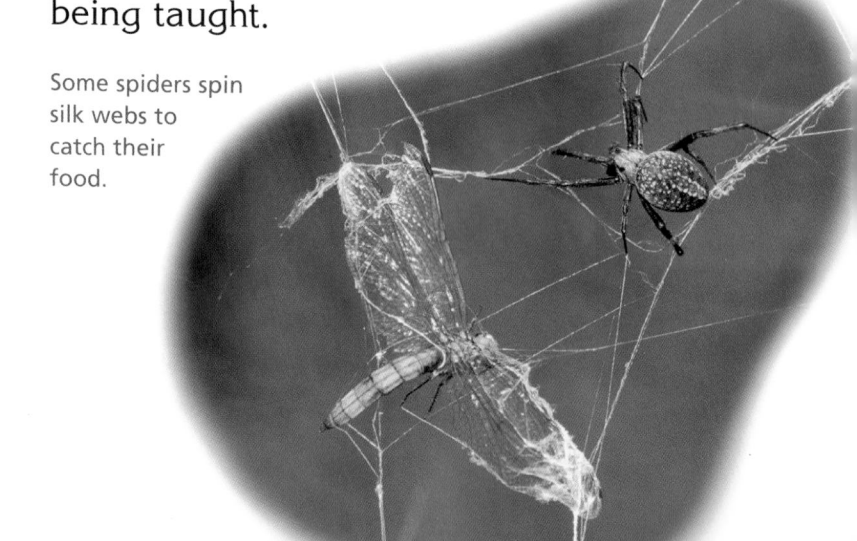

Some spiders spin silk webs to catch their food.

Glossary

abdomen the back part of a spider's body

arachnid a member of a group of animals including spiders, with eight legs and two main body parts

ballooning a method of travel by which spiderlings are carried by the wind on threads of silk

cephalothorax the front part of a spider's body made up of the head and chest

dragline a silk thread spiders spin behind themselves

molt to shed the outer skin

prey an animal that is hunted and taken as food by another animal

signal thread a silk thread that goes between a spider and its web. It shakes when prey is caught in the web and serves as a signal to the spider.

spiderling a newly hatched spider

spinneret a small organ at the end of a spider's abdomen used to spin silk